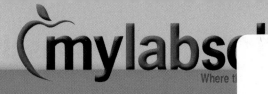

MW00356479

From watching actual classroom video footage of teachers and students interacting to building standards-based lessons and web-based portfolios . . . from a robust resource library of the "What Every Teacher Should Know About" series to complete instruction on writing an effective re-search paper . . . **MyLabSchool** brings together an amazing collection of resources for future teachers. This website gives you a wealth of videos, print and simulated cases, career advice, and much more.

Use **MyLabSchool** with this Allyn and Bacon Education text, and you will have everything you need to succeed in your course. Assignment IDs have also been incorporated into many Allyn and Bacon Education texts to link to the online material in **MyLabSchool** . . . connecting the teachers of tomorrow to the information they need today.

VISIT www.mylabschool.com **to learn more about this invaluable resource and Take a Tour!**

Here's what you'll find in mylabschool
Where the classroom comes to life!

VideoLab ▶

Access hundreds of video clips of actual classroom situations from a variety of grade levels and school settings. These 3- to 5-minute closed-captioned video clips illustrate real teacher–student interaction, and are organized both topically *and* by discipline. Students can test their knowledge of class-room concepts with integrated observation questions.

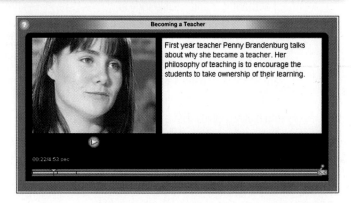

◀ Lesson & Portfolio Builder

This feature enables students to create, main-tain, update, and share online portfolios and standards-based lesson plans. The Lesson Planner walks students, step-by-step, through the process of creating a complete lesson plan, including verifiable objectives, assessments, and related state standards. Upon comple-tion, the lesson plan can be printed, saved, e-mailed, or uploaded to a website.

Here's what you'll find in mylabschool™

Where the classroom comes to life!

Simulations ▶

This area of MyLabSchool contains interactive tools designed to better prepare future teachers to provide an appropriate education to students with special needs. To achieve this goal, the IRIS (IDEA and Research for Inclusive Settings) Center at Vanderbilt University has created course enhancement materials. These resources include online interactive modules, case study units, information briefs, student activities, an online dictionary, and a searchable directory of disability-related web sites.

◀ Resource Library

MyLabSchool includes a collection of PDF files on crucial and timely topics within education. Each topic is applicable to any education class, and these documents are ideal resources to prepare students for the challenges they will face in the classroom. This resource can be used to reinforce a central topic of the course, or to enhance coverage of a topic you need to explore in more depth.

Research Navigator ▶

This comprehensive research tool gives users access to four exclusive databases of authoritative and reliable source material. It offers a comprehensive, step-by-step walk-through of the research process. In addition, students can view sample research papers and consult guidelines on how to prepare endnotes and bibliographies. The latest release also features a new bibliography-maker program—AutoCite.

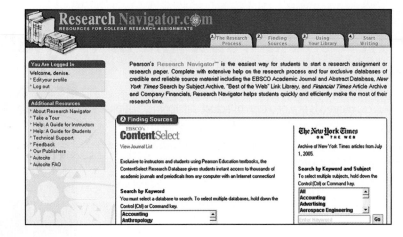

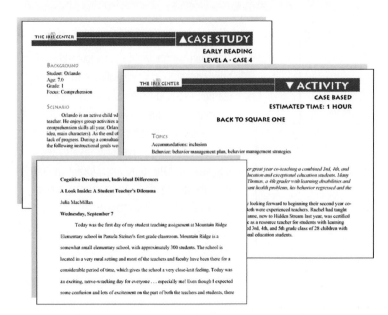

◀ Case Archive

This collection of print and simulated cases can be easily accessed by topic and subject area, and can be integrated into your course. The cases are drawn from Allyn & Bacon's best-selling books, and represent the complete range of disciplines and student ages. It's an ideal way to consider and react to real classroom scenarios. The possibilities for using these high-quality cases within the course are endless.

DEAR COLLEAGUES,

Educational psychology never stands still, but these days it is changing at a dizzying pace. In particular, No Child Left Behind is changing practices in U.S. schools in fundamental ways, and educational psychology has had to run to keep up, providing the evidence base for many of the practices schools are being asked to adopt. Instruction, accountability, assessment, accommodations to individual needs, technology applications, and other central aspects of education all have to be re-examined in light of the new pressures on schools and the new opportunities to address longstanding problems. The rapid increase in numbers of English language learners in U.S. schools and new research on how to help these students succeed is another area of great and timely importance.

Traditionally, educational psychology textbooks are revised every three years. Usually, that's often enough to represent the developments in research and theory in educational psychology itself. However, in the current context, three years is too long to wait. New policy developments have already made parts of my eighth edition obsolete, and exciting progress in research and development are opening up new vistas, which students of educational psychology need to know about. Those who are or soon will be practicing educators will particularly need up-to-date information to prepare them to understand the changes happening in education and in educational psychology.

In response, I have written an additional chapter for the eighth edition of *Educational Psychology: Theory, Research, and Practice,* making it sort of an "Edition 8½." This new Chapter 15 focuses in particular on NCLB, how it is working in practice, where it seems to be working, and where it is not. Closely connected to this, I've discussed new concerns about how inappropriate uses of assessment can distort outcomes, and how benchmark assessments and data-driven reform can build on the accountability movement to benefit children. I've reviewed new research on effective programs and practices for English language learners, a group of increasing size and importance across the U.S. I've also discussed new research on non-school solutions to learning problems, such as dealing with vision, hearing, and nutrition problems, and presented exciting uses of technology that are transforming teaching. Finally, the chapter updates research on the brain, an area of great interest and importance in educational psychology today.

In the introduction to the first edition of *Educational Psychology,* I said that my purpose was to write a text so down-to-earth that the readers could almost "smell the broccoli cooking in the school cafeteria." I've kept that purpose in all editions of my text, and in my additional chapter as well. It's important to know about Piaget and Vygotsky, but when your students become teachers and leaders in education, they'll also need a deep understanding of today's issues of policy and practice. Developments in the technology of book publishing have made it possible to update textbooks more frequently, and in the rapidly changing environment of today, I wanted to use this new opportunity to help you prepare your students for the world they'll face.

—Bob Slavin

EIGHTH EDITION

EDUCATIONAL PSYCHOLOGY

Theory and Practice

Chapter 15   Current Issues and Emerging Trends

Robert E. Slavin
Johns Hopkins University

PEARSON

Boston   New York   San Francisco
Mexico City   Montreal   Toronto   London   Madrid   Munich   Paris
Hong Kong   Singapore   Tokyo   Cape Town   Sydney

Senior Series Editor: Arnis E. Burvikovs
Series Editorial Assistant: Erin E. Reilly
Marketing Manager: Erica DeLuca
Production Editor: Annette Joseph
Editorial Production Service: Omegatype Typography, Inc.
Composition Buyer: Linda Cox
Manufacturing Buyer: Megan Cochran
Electronic Composition: Omegatype Typography, Inc.
Interior Design: Omegatype Typography, Inc.
Photo Researcher: Naomi Rudov
Cover Administrator: Kristina Mose-Libon

For related titles and support materials, visit our online catalog at www.ablongman.com.

Copyright © 2008 Pearson Education, Inc.

Between the time website information is gathered and then published, it is not unusual for some sites to have closed. Also, the transcription of URLs can result in typographical errors. The publisher would appreciate notification where these errors occur so that they may be corrected in subsequent editions.

ISBN 0-205-54016-3

978-0-205-54016-7

Printed in the United States of America

10 9 8 7 6 5 4 3 2   CIN   11 10 09 08 07

Photo credits: p. vi: Christina Kennedy/PhotoEdit; p. 3: Robin Sachs/PhotoEdit; p. 7: Jose L. Pelaez/The Stock Market/Corbis; p. 12: Spencer Grant/PhotoEdit; p. 15: A. Ramey/PhotoEdit

Contents

Current Issues and Emerging Trends

*R*obert Milder walks the halls of the elementary school on the south side of Chicago where he is principal—a school that had been identified as failing before his arrival. He had come with the mission of raising overall test scores—and he's managed to do that, bringing the school's scores above the failing rate and erasing that designation from next to its name in just two short years. To make that happen, Robert has focused on two things. First, he has tried to develop a faculty that is responsive to the needs of their students. He has scoured the pool of new teachers throughout the system to find those with energy, commitment, and skills for working in a challenging environment. The new energy in the building is almost tangible as Robert walks the corridors. And second, Robert has hunted down money from every source he can find; he scrounges funds for projects that teachers deem important—and he knows that they are spending their own money for their own projects. Robert knows that the turn-around in test scores will enhance the confidence of his young teachers. But in the long run, he's not so sure. How long can he and his teachers continue to work this hard? And just what are the limits of improvement for these students, whose home environments reward them very little for success in school? And what about all this testing? Legislation such as No Child Left Behind is all well and good when it focuses attention and funding on schools. But just what does it mean for his kids to be scoring higher on tests? Does that really mean they'll be better thinkers, better problem-solvers? What does this focus on test scores say to these kids about the real world?

The last time the field of educational psychology really saw a "sea change" in the content it covered was probably in the 1980s, with the emergence of cognitive learning theories based on the work of Piaget and Vygotsky. But what is happening now, in the first decade of the 21st century, may eventually be seen as just as powerful. The changes are political (the emergence of the federal government as a more active player in U.S. public education); social (the rise in the numbers of English language learners; the continued achievement gap between races); and scientific (new knowledge about how brains function that may eventually force us to look at learning through new lenses; the increasing impact of technology in the classroom). In addition, we are seeing the shadow of accountability spread over almost every decision that educators make, and, as a result, a tremendous increase in benchmark assessments and in data-driven reform.

*N*O CHILD LEFT BEHIND: FIVE YEARS OF FEDERAL ACTIVISM

In December 2001, the U.S. Congress passed the No Child Left Behind Act (NCLB), which has significantly changed the landscape of American education. The intent of NCLB was to close the achievement gap between students, particularly the gap between those from middle-class homes and those from disadvantaged homes. NCLB, which has specific provisions covering reading instruction, instruction for English language learners, and the need to rely on "evidence-based" or "scientifically based" practices, promised to transform educational practice by mandating test-based accountability, requiring annual testing in grades 3–8, introducing new sanctions for schools not making "adequate yearly progress," insisting that all teachers have adequate levels of qualification, and much more.

The Ten "Big Effects"

In the years since its passage, what changes has No Child Left Behind actually caused? What impact has it had? Jack Jennings and Diane Stark Rentner (2006) drew on surveys conducted by the Center for Education Policy, an independent nonprofit research and advocacy organization, to describe ten "big effects" of NCLB on U.S. public education. These are not always what we might have anticipated.

1. **State and district officials report rising achievement on state tests, but it is not clear if this is meaningful.**

   According to Jennings and Rentner, three-quarters of state and district officials indicate that their state test scores in reading and math have been going up and that achievement gaps are narrowing. However, state test scores in most states have been increasing for the last twenty years, while the National Assessment of Academic Progress (NAEP) remains little changed, especially in reading.

   Bottom line: Any achievement effects attributable to NCLB cannot be determined yet.

> **ON THE WEB**
>
> For more details about No Child Left Behind, see the U.S. Department of Education website **www.ed.gov/nclb**.

2. **Schools are spending more time on reading and math, sometimes at the expense of subjects not tested.**

NCLB's emphasis on reading and math has meant less time devoted to other subjects in most schools.

Because NCLB accountability focuses only on reading and math (although mandated science testing will be added in 2007), many schools (71%, according to Jennings & Rentner) are reducing time in other subjects, in particular social studies. Virtually all high-poverty districts have mandated a specific amount of time for reading instruction; around 55% of non-poverty districts have done the same. Even before NCLB, we had seen a reduction of time for "specials" such as art, music, and physical education, primarily for budgetary reasons.

Bottom line: Achievement in subjects beyond those being tested regularly is likely to be suffering under NCLB.

3. Schools are paying much more attention to test scores and alignment of curriculum to tests.

Predictably, school leaders are learning to watch their test scores carefully and, particularly where a school has not met the "adequate yearly progress" (AYP) standard for two years or more, are making modifications to curriculum and instruction to more closely align these with the testing program. More and more, we are likely to see educational decisions being made based on testing data, especially decisions about how to improve results. As NCLB matures and more schools do not meet the AYP requirements for several years, more and more schools are likely to look to testing data as a basis for making decisions about improvement.

Bottom line: Schools are modifying curriculum and instruction to teach to tests, particularly schools that are identified as not meeting "adequate yearly progress" requirements. This requirement is likely to have increasing impact in the coming decade.

4. Low-performing schools are undergoing makeovers rather than radical restructuring.

NCLB requires that schools that fail to make adequate yearly progress for five years be "restructured." It was anticipated that such schools would make major changes, from adopting new schoolwide reform models to complete reconstitution, or would be taken over by states, dissolved, or turned into charter schools. For the most part, this has not happened yet. Instead, most schools continue to muddle through, making modest improvements in hope of better luck next time. This may be attributable at least in part to a lack of funding to support such changes.

Under NCLB, students in schools in need of improvement were supposed to be able to transfer to more successful schools. According to Jennings and Rentner, this is generally not happening; only 2% of eligible students have transferred to new schools. Students in schools in need of improvement are also eligible for "supplemental educational services," usually after-school instruction in small groups. Only 20% of eligible students are taking advantage of these services. School leaders are skeptical about the benefits of both of these remedies.

Bottom line: NCLB has not yet caused a major restructuring of schools—although it is certainly impacting the day-to-day life of learning and instruction.

CONNECTIONS

For more on the No Child Left Behind Act, see Ch. 9, pp. 305–306.

5. Teachers have made progress in demonstrating academic qualifications.

More than 88% of school districts report that all of their teachers of core academic subjects meet the NCLB definition of "highly qualified," but they still have problems in areas such as high school math and special education. However, district leaders express doubt that the "highly qualified" standards will actually improve teaching.

Bottom line: The NCLB definition of "highly qualified" may not jibe completely with what makes an effective teacher.

6. Students are taking a lot more tests.

To comply with NCLB, all states must test annually in grades 3–8, plus one high school year (usually 11). Nineteen states had mandated reading and math tests in all grades, 3–8, in 2002; most states had only tested in selected grades. In 2007–2008, science tests will be added to the list. In addition, pressure to improve end-of-year test scores has led to the rapidly increasing use of benchmark assessments, tests given 3 to 5 times per year to give educators information about how well their students are likely to do on state assessments. (See the discussion of *benchmark assessments* later in this chapter.)

Bottom line: Most students are spending more time being prepped for, and taking, standardized tests than ever before.

7. Schools are paying much more attention to the achievement of particular groups of students.

Under NCLB, schools are held accountable for the achievement of each of several subgroups of students: African American, Hispanic, and White; students in special education; and low-income students. Because of this, school leaders report paying a lot more attention to the scores of each group—scores that formerly might have been hidden in an overall group average. This provision of NCLB has drawn considerable praise but has also led to a great deal of controversy about assessment of students with disabilities and of English language learners, and it has not yet led to any decrease in the achievement gap between disadvantaged and minority students and middle-class and white students, as is discussed later in this chapter. States and districts have expressed repeated frustration with requirements that they administer the state tests to students with disabilities, who may not be able to perform well on them under any circumstances, and NCLB did modify the rules to allow a small proportion of students to be excluded.

Bottom line: NCLB has caused greater discussion about the performance and assessment of students in all subgroups.

8. The percentage of schools on state "needs improvement" lists has remained steady but has not grown.

About 10% of all schools have been designated as being "in need of improvement," which means that they have not met their "adequate yearly progress" goals for two years in a row. Schools with this designation are required to provide school choice or tutoring services. This number has leveled off in most states, with different schools going on and off the list each year. However, states vary widely in the percentages of schools meeting standards because of substantial differences in the difficulty of their tests and their procedures for computing adequate yearly progress.

Bottom line: Differences in state standards make the identification of "needs improvement" schools hard to define.

9. The federal government is playing a bigger role in education.

According to the U.S. Constitution, education is a state responsibility, and by tradition it is a local responsibility. NCLB has enormously increased the federal role in education at all levels, as the U.S. Department of Education oversees the state testing programs and strictly enforces the provisions of NCLB. In addition, much of the implementation of NCLB has been handed to the states, whose role has traditionally been secondary to that of local districts.

Bottom line: The interactions of state, local, and federal authorities in the U.S. have changed significantly as a result of NCLB.

10. Under NCLB, states and districts have expanded roles in the operation of individual schools, but inadequate funds to carry out their new duties.

State departments of education have increased responsibilities to monitor compliance with NCLB and to help schools and districts in need of improvement. Districts also have an increased role—they must administer many more tests, direct more attention to schools that need improvement, and make judgments about whether or not teachers are "highly qualified." However, neither states nor districts have received sufficient funding to perform their new roles adequately. In 2005, 36 of 50 states reported that they did not have sufficient staff to implement NCLB's requirements, and in both 2004 and 2005, 80% of local districts reported that they were now absorbing costs for NCLB mandates for which federal funds have not been provided. In fact, federal funding has stagnated or decreased over the last few years, and two-thirds of U.S. school districts have received no increases—or have even lost ground—in federal funding. At the same time, NCLB has led to diminished authority and autonomy for principals and school staffs, while increasing district and state authority.

Bottom line: Without adequate funding, the implementation of NCLB has left states and districts with additional expenses and schools with less autonomy.

ON THE WEB

For more on the Center for Education Policy's surveys of No Child Left Behind, see **www.cep-dc.org**. For criticisms of NCLB, see **http://nochildleft.com**.

No Child Left Behind is greatly increasing accountability pressures on schools, districts, and states. It remains to be seen whether this will truly be beneficial to students. The U.S. Department of Education is claiming successes, but the National Assessment of Educational Progress scores have shown no genuine improvements. Until this happens, we will not have any reliable basis for saying that NCLB is working, and even then there will be questions about what was lost to produce gains in reading and math scores.

After-School and Summer School Programs: Additional Time Can Support Progress

Partly as a result of NCLB, which pushes schools to make annual progress in overall achievement, as well as federal funding for this purpose, districts and schools are increasingly offering after-school and summer school programs intended to help at-risk students improve their academic achievement. A recent review by Lauer, Akiba, Wilkerson, Apthorp, Snow, and Martin-Glenn (2006) looked at the research on these out-of-school programs. They found small positive effects of out-of-school programs for reading and math when children who attended these programs were compared to those who did not. When the programs included tutoring, however, effects were much more positive. Effects were the same for after-school as for summer-school programs, suggesting that progress can be made even when formal school is not in session. The importance of these findings is that they indicate that struggling children can be helped by extending instructional time for them, especially if the additional time is used for targeted instructional activities.

For more on summer school, see Cooper, Charlton, Valentine, & Muhlenbruck (2000). For more on after school, see McComb & Scott-Little (2003).

$\mathcal{A}$CCOUNTABILITY: THE PRESSURE TO MEASURE PROGRESS

Primarily because of NCLB, but also in response to a general sense of disappointment with public education in the U.S. over the past several decades, accountability has become the primary "hot button" for public education in general: States must be accountable for the results of their school districts; districts for the results of their individual schools; principals for the results achieved by their teachers; and teachers for the results achieved by their students. But what **accountability** really means is sometimes controversial. What measures actually reflect real progress? Do statewide tests do that? Do we need more instruments to measure what our children are learning?

The "Contamination" of Accountability

As McGill-Franzen and Allington (2006) point out, the U.S. Department of Education has implemented high-stakes achievement testing as "the nearly singular approach to accountability" (762). If these tests are our only available measure, what happens if they become contaminated? McGill-Franzen and Allington suggest that exactly this may be happening, precisely because of the magnified pressure for accountability central to NCLB. They document several types of potential contamination (also see Popham, 2005).

1. Flunking and Retention   **Retention** rates have risen dramatically in recent years. Texas held back 12,000 third graders recently, Florida held back 24,000, New York City failed 16,000 third graders, and Miami had 2,000 students in third grade for the third time.

There is considerable debate about whether retention in grade is good or bad for low-achieving students. Most research finds it harmful (e.g., Shepard & Smith, 1989). But whatever its impact on individual students, it is clear that a dramatic increase in retention changes the meaning of assessment systems. Third-grade norms are based on the assumption that the children taking the tests are approximately nine years old. Holding students back means that a lot of ten- and eleven-year-olds are taking the test.

Imagine, for example, that a Miami nine-year-old scores 20% on a state reading test in third grade and is retained. The next year, he scores 40%, and he is retained again. Now he is eleven years old, and the third time, he scores 60%. Has he improved? Not in any real sense. But his increases (which are due to two things: his get-

accountability
Responsibility of educators to the public to show that their students are making good progress, especially on test scores and other quantitative measures of performance.

retention
Keeping a student in the same grade for a second or third year based on failure to achieve certain academic goals.

ting older, and his repeating instruction in the test content multiple times) look like test score gains for third-graders. Keep in mind also that his former classmates are taking the fifth grade test by now. If the student had been passed each year, he might well be scoring 20% in fifth grade, too. But because he has been retained, the fifth grade scores do not include his—and they are incrementally higher as a result. That student's district and state can proudly report these gains to the media. But the student has probably not been helped at all. In fact, research shows that within a few years, the scores of students who were retained tend to fall back to the bottom of the pile.

This return to flunking is an expensive non-solution, but more important in this world of high-stakes testing, it produces an overestimate of school effectiveness, as McGill-Franzen and Allington point out, inflating reported achievement.

2. Test Preparation   Accountability pressure causes many schools to spend a lot of time teaching students how to take tests. Up to a point, there is nothing wrong with helping students know how to be strategic test-takers, but in some schools "test prep" goes on all the time, pushing out more important learning. Endless hours are spent responding to practice tests in the format that state tests will take; after-school preparation sessions are offered to borderline students (or, in some districts, to all students). Very little time is devoted to critical thinking or problem-solving—or, for that matter, the basic communication skills that students will most need to succeed outside the testing environment.

The pressure for accountability and the huge increase in mandated, standardized tests has led to many unanticipated consequences.

There is some evidence that test prep can improve performance on tests. But there is no evidence that this kind of endless test prep improves students' actual proficiency in, for example, reading—one of the skills being most frequently tested. Excessive test prep is, then, another form of contamination of accountability; if, as McGill-Franzen and Allington argue, test prep "improves test performance without actually improving proficiencies, then the accountability system will report contaminated information, and policy makers will make bad decisions" (765).

CONNECTIONS

For more on standardized testing in general, see Ch. 14.

3. Inappropriate Accommodations for Students with Disabilities   Because students in special education have to make adequate yearly progress gains if their schools are to escape NCLB sanctions, educators are especially concerned about the performance of students who have been classified with disabilities. No Child Left Behind allows for appropriate accommodations for students with disabilities, but when the test is of reading skills, and the accommodation is that the test is read aloud to the child, then the test is hardly assessing the ability to read. There are many documented cases of this kind of inappropriate accommodation, with the result that students who read poorly, or indeed cannot read at all, are measured as proficient readers. Clearly the NCLB goal of ensuring that students with disabilities are not "left behind" is a noble one, but designing appropriate measures to account for their progress is not so simple.

Benchmark Assessments

In test-obsessed American schools, you'd think the last thing we'd need is more tests. Yet from coast to coast, the hottest innovation going is just that: benchmark assessments that assess children three, five, or even eight times a year, usually in reading and math.

benchmark assessments

Tests given several times a year to give educators early information on student performance so that they can take corrective action before state accountability testing.

The popularity of **benchmark assessments** is easy to understand. No Child Left Behind (NCLB) has increased the already substantial pressure on schools to improve scores on their state tests. Yet state tests are given too infrequently and the scores arrive too late to be of much use in adjusting instructional policies or practices. For example, most states test in the spring. By the time scores are reported, it is summer or fall. A school might find out in July that its math scores are in trouble. Yet by July, schools have already committed their resources and made their plans for the coming year. Information from fourth-grade test scores, for example, cannot benefit the fourth graders who took the test, and may be too late to be of much value to the next group of fourth graders as well.

Educators have long understood this problem and have long looked for solutions. In the 1970s, Benjamin Bloom's (1976) mastery learning strategies depended on "formative assessments," low-stakes tests to tell teachers whether or not their students are headed toward mastery of "summative assessments." Today, a wide array of benchmark assessments designed to give educators useful early information on students' progress are available. Many districts and even individual teachers have designed and used their own benchmark assessments. Benchmark assessments allow educators to identify how each student, class, subgroup, and school is doing on each of the objectives assessed by the state and emphasized in state and district standards, so they can target professional development and reform where they are needed most.

Types of Benchmark Assessments   Educators use a broad range of benchmark assessments. Table 15.1 shows some of the most important ways in which benchmark assessments differ.

Online vs. Paper-and-Scanner.   In the past, benchmark assessments have primarily used paper tests, often with optical scanners to assist with scoring. However, as computers become more common in schools, online assessment is also becoming common. Online assessment usually involves moving kids to computer labs or computers to kids (as in Computers on Wheels, or COWs). Online testing can save time in scoring and collating scores.

However students take their tests, most benchmark systems produce computerized score reports that enable teachers and administrators to "slice and dice" the data many ways, to provide information on subtests, subgroups of children, classes, students who are near state cut points, and so on.

Frequent vs. Infrequent Assessment.   Most benchmark assessments are given four to five times per year, but some are given only three times and some as often as monthly. Typically, they take one hour each for reading and math.

Table 15.1		
Attributes of Benchmark Assessments		
Online	*vs.*	*Paper-Plus-Scanner*
Frequent (up to 8 times/year)	vs.	Infrequent (3 times/year)
Repeated Measures of All State Standards	vs.	Skill by Skill
State-Specific	vs.	National
Teacher-Created	vs.	District/School Selected

Repeated Measures vs. Skill-by-Skill.   One major dimension on which benchmark approaches vary is whether they focus on the specific skills expected to be taught by a given point in the year or whether they are repeated measures of all skills expected in that grade level. For example, a skill-by-skill math benchmark might focus on fractions in November, decimals in January, geometry in March, and problem solving in May. In contrast, a repeated assessment benchmark would test all skills each time.

Skill-by-skill assessments serve as pacing guides, giving teachers and schools detailed information on students' learning of the curriculum they have been taught. However, they do not allow teachers or administrators to predict how students will do on their state tests, and for this reason skill-by-skill assessments are generally giving way to repeated measures of all skills. Repeated measures, on the other hand, are designed to parallel state assessments and each other, so educators can closely monitor progress toward success on state assessments. Of course, benchmark assessments do not replace curriculum-based classroom measures (e.g., unit tests), given much more frequently.

State-Specific or National.   Historically, commercially available benchmark assessments were national (one set of tests was used everywhere) and only district- or teacher-made benchmark assessments were specific to state standards. As accountability pressure based on state tests has increased, benchmarks are increasingly being developed specifically for each state.

Teacher-Created vs. District/School Selected.   Several benchmark systems provide teachers and administrators with a large computerized pool of items keyed to a set of objectives and (usually) to state standards. Teachers can use this to create their own classroom tests and to check students' progress on state standards, and administrators at the school or district level can use the same procedures to create common assessments. This gives local educators more control over the process and more alignment with their curriculum, but it does not allow for close correlation with state assessments.

ON THE WEB

For more on benchmark assessments, see **www.nwea.org,** and **www.successforall. org/ayp/4sight.htm.**

Benchmark assessments can allow schools to take their achievement "pulse," but as in medicine, taking a pulse does not constitute a cure. It's what the doctor and patient do next that matters. Similarly, a benchmark assessment tells schools where they're headed and where they need to focus, but use of benchmark assessments has not yet been shown in itself to increase student achievement.

Benchmark assessments are useful tools in the hands of enlightened educators, but they are nothing more than indicators of children's current achievement. As part of a comprehensive strategy for district and school reform, benchmark assessments can play a key supporting role, but only a supporting role. If we're going to take even more of our children's precious class time for testing, we must use the results intelligently and proactively to improve core teaching and learning.

Data-Driven Reform

data-driven reform

A strategy for school reform in which educators continually collect and analyze data on student performance to guide instructional decisions.

The movement toward using benchmark assessments is part of a broader trend toward using data to drive reforms in schools and districts in general, as we mentioned in the first part of this chapter. **Data-driven reform** goes beyond just looking at scores on state tests. School leaders involved in such reforms organize information from state tests and benchmark assessments by subskill, subgroup, grade level, and other categories, and add information on attendance, dropouts, programs in use in schools, and so on to find "root causes" for the school's problems. They then carefully consider potential solutions to their problems, ideally programs with strong evidence of effectiveness, implement those solutions, and then continue to monitor benchmark and test data to see that they are working.

Heritage & Chen (2005) discuss an approach to data-driven reform that uses a web-based tool called the Quality School Portfolio (QSP) to help school leaders organize and make sense of data. They then describe a process for using data to guide school reform:

1. **Determine what you want to know.** Data-based reform should begin with a problem that the educators involved want to solve, or a question they want answered. No one pays attention to data that do not tell them something they want to know.

2. **Collect data.** Educators involved in data-based reform organize existing data and collect new data to answer the questions they posed. The data could include state and benchmark tests, additional assessments (such as writing or math problem-solving assessments not part of the state test), information on materials and programs being used by teachers, teachers' and students' attitudes, or whatever else might inform decisions about reforms being considered (Bernhardt, 2003).

3. **Analyze results.** The next step is to organize the data, first just computing averages and then using the data to test ideas about what is causing the problems the school is trying to solve. For example, imagine that a school has lower math scores than it likes. A school committee reviews the state test scores and quarterly benchmark scores, and they all tell the same story: scores are low, and not improving. Could it be that the teachers are not focusing on all skills tested? The committee looks at scores on portions of the test (e.g, fractions, geometry, word problems) and finds that the scores are low across the board. Could the problem be isolated to certain subgroups? The committee looks at scores for boys and girls, African Americans, Hispanics, and Whites. They see one surprising pattern: girls seem to be doing particularly poorly. The committee arranges to visit classes and see what is happening. When they return to discuss their findings, they have a whole new perspective on the data. Teachers throughout the school are making extensive use of traditional lectures and problem solving, as suggested by their textbooks.

In many classes, an aggressive group of boys dominates the discussions, while most girls are bored and feel left out of the class activities. They found classes in which most girls never participated and did not say a single thing in a 50-minute lesson. Linking their quantitative data with their observations, the committee decided that the problem might be that teaching methods were not engaging all students.

4. **Set priorities and goals.** In data-based reform, it is not enough to know the data. The school must take action based on the data. This begins with setting priorities and goals for solutions the school might try. The goals should be measurable, focused on student achievement, realistic, and attainable (Schmoker, 1999). In the case of the school with the math problem, the committee set a goal of improving the math performance of all students, with a particular focus on the girls, and set up a plan to closely monitor quarterly benchmark data.

5. **Develop strategies.** The most important step in data-driven reform is to develop specific strategies to solve identified problems. School leaders need to consider potential solutions for the problems they have observed. For example, to solve an achievement problem, the school might look at the federal What Works Clearinghouse (2006; www.whatworks.ed.gov) or the Best Evidence Encyclopedia (Center for Data-Driven Reform in Education, 2006; www.bestevidence.org), both of which summarize scientific reviews of research on educational programs for grades pre-K to 12.

In the case of the school with the math problem, committee members looked at the Best Evidence Encyclopedia (2006) and found that there was good evidence for cooperative learning in elementary math. They reasoned that this could increase the participation of all students. They found a local trainer who trained the teachers to use cooperative learning in math, and over time, they began to see their math benchmark scores improve. In classroom visits, committee members saw students, including girls, much more engaged in math lessons, talking actively about their current understandings. Later, when the state test scores came back, the committee was glad to see that math scores had improved for all students, but especially for girls.

ON THE WEB

For educator-friendly summaries of research evidence on pre-K–12 programs, see:
What Works Clearinghouse: **www.whatworks.ed.gov**
Best Evidence Encyclopedia: **www.bestevidence.org**

For more on data-driven reform, see:
Center for Data-Driven Reform in Education: **www.cddre.org**
Center for Research on Evaluation, Standards, and Student Testing (CRESST):
www.cse.ucla.edu

WHY THE ACHIEVEMENT GAP ISN'T CLOSING, AND HOW WE CAN HELP

Five years after the passage of NCLB, an explicit goal of which is the closing of the achievement gap between middle-class students and their disadvantaged classmates, recent studies show no significant change. A study released in November 2006, by the Northwest Evaluation Association (NWEA) indicates that, for every group at every grade, students from poor schools "grew less than students from wealthy schools, and minority students exhibited less growth than their non-minority peers" (NWEA,

2006). In general, according to this study of over 550,000 students in reading and just under that in math, African American and Hispanic students enrolled in high-poverty schools start school with lower skills, and lose more ground in every grade—both by growing less academically during the school year and by losing more of their skills over the summer—than their peers from wealthier, whiter schools. Similar studies by NWEA since NCLB was passed show steady improvement of students overall, as measured by mandated standardized tests, but no closing of the "growth" gap between well-to-do white students and their less affluent peers of color.

What seems clear, then, is that NCLB has not yet made progress in closing the achievement gap. Do programs or approaches exist that may prove useful in this area? Research suggests that there are, but these are not yet widely used.

Effective Instruction for English Language Learners

School districts throughout the U.S. and Canada are experiencing rates of immigration that are approaching the extraordinary levels of the early 20th century. As a result, schools everywhere are having to learn how to teach children who enter the school with English language skills not sufficient to succeed in English-only instruction.

A major development in research on English-language learners is the publication in 2006 of the report of the National Literacy Panel on Language-Minority Children and Youth (the NLC, for short) (August & Shanahan, 2006a). The NLC was commissioned by the U.S. Department of Education to follow up on the influential National Reading Panel (NRP, 2000), which reviewed research on reading but did not consider issues relating to English language learners in any depth. NLC members, distinguished researchers from many backgrounds, reviewed research on English language learners. Some of their major conclusions are as follows.

CONNECTIONS

For more on English language learners, see Ch. 4, pp. 113–116.

Language of Instruction The NLC concluded that language-minority students instructed in their native language as well as English perform, on average, better on English reading measures than language-minority students instructed only in English. This is consistent with the conclusions of a review by Slavin & Cheung (2005), which

The huge increase in English language learners in American classrooms is expected to continue despite pressure to slow immigration, and educators continue to look for effective approaches to instruction.

found that Spanish-dominant English language learners taught to read in both Spanish and English (at different times of the day) ended up reading English better than children taught only in English.

Effective Programs   Shanahan & Beck (2006) identified several studies that evaluated a variety of approaches to improving the reading performance of English language learners. They concluded that there were positive effects on reading performance of the Success for All comprehensive school reform program (Slavin & Madden, 2001), and they found benefits of cooperative learning, tutoring, and captioned TV (also see Cheung & Slavin, 2005).

Vocabulary   Snow (2006) noted that while there was good evidence for the effectiveness of various approaches for many aspects of reading, there was less known about how to improve the English vocabularies of ELLs. Promising practices with Spanish-dominant students include using Spanish words as synonyms in vocabulary instruction, and providing extensive opportunities to discuss English vocabulary in cooperative groups (August & Shanahan, 2006b).

Also see Hill & Flynn (2006) for descriptions of approaches to the instruction of English language learners.

ON THE WEB

See a review of research on effective reading programs for English language learners at **www.bestevidence.org/_images/word_docs/ELL_fullreport.pdf**.

Non-School Solutions to Achievement Problems of Disadvantaged Children

In a 2004 book, Richard Rothstein makes an important set of observations about the gaps in achievement between middle-class and disadvantaged children. He notes that major explanations for the gap come from problems not generally under the control of schools, which could be rectified by enlightened policies. Some of the examples he suggests are surprising. These include a variety of physical disabilities and healthcare shortfalls, all of which occur at much higher rates in children of poverty than in their wealthier peers.

Vision   Rothstein notes that poor children have severe vision impairment at twice the normal rate. Surprisingly, juvenile delinquents are found to have extraordinarily high rates of vision problems. Rothstein cites data indicating that more than 50% of minority and low-income children have vision problems that interfere with their academic work. Some require eyeglasses, and others need eye-exercise therapies. A study by Harris (2002) found that disadvantaged fourth graders who received free eyeglasses and therapy gained substantially relative to a control group. Children in school are usually screened for nearsightedness, but not for farsightedness or tracking (Gould & Gould, 2003). Compounding this problem is that, even when low-income children have prescriptions for glasses, they often do not obtain them, do not wear them to school, or do not replace them when they break.

Hearing   Rothstein cites evidence that disadvantaged children have more hearing problems than middle-class children, due in particular to a failure to get medical care for ear infections. Accommodations for moderate hearing problems are rarely made, so many children simply experience school as frustrating because they can hear some but not all of the instruction.

Lead Exposure   Disadvantaged children are far more likely to live in homes where dust from old lead paint is in the air. Even small amounts of lead can lead to loss of cognitive functioning and hearing loss. Studies have found blood lead levels of poor children to be five times those of middle-class children (Brooks-Gunn & Duncan, 1997; GAO, 1999).

Asthma   Poor, urban children have remarkably high rates of asthma. Studies in New York and Chicago (Whitman, Williams, & Shah, 2004) found that one in four inner-city African American children had asthma, six times the national rate. In turn, asthma is a major cause of chronic school absence, and even when in school, untreated asthma interferes with academic performance.

General Medical Care   Disadvantaged children are much less likely to receive adequate medical care than are middle-class children, and this leads to problems with absenteeism, poor motivation due to poor health, and vision, hearing, and asthma problems mentioned earlier (Starfield, 1997).

Nutrition   While serious malnutrition is rare in the U.S., under-nutrition is common among poor children, and this affects academic performance. One study (Neisser et al., 1996) found that simply giving children vitamin and mineral supplements improved their test scores.

Rothstein's (2004) argument is that these and other aspects of poverty could be solved, and doing so could have a significant impact on the achievement of low-income children. Even though there are health agencies and social service agencies that are charged with solving these problems, schools have the advantage that they see the children every day. Simple reforms, such as improving school lunches or providing free eyeglasses that stay at school, might be as effective as much more expensive interventions, such as tutoring or special education, which may not be addressing the root causes of children's problems.

*E*MERGING APPLICATIONS OF TECHNOLOGY

The area of educational change that may be most obvious even to the casual observer is the integration of new technological applications into the classroom. From issuing laptop computers to every student, as some colleges and even K–12 schools do, to employing sophisticated adaptive technology to support students with disabilities, to requiring PowerPoint presentations from sixth graders, to using MP3 downloads for study review, new applications of technology continue to appear in education.

New approaches to educational simulations, in which students take on roles within simulated environments, appear to have promise (Dede, 2006), and are often very popular with students. Voice-recognition applications in which students read to computers, which can recognize their errors, give them feedback, and pose question for clarification at strategic points within the text, also appear to add value to the educational process (Adams, 2006; Beck & Mostow, 2005; Mostow, 2006).

ON THE WEB

For more on innovative technologies, see: **www.muve.gse.harvard/rivercityproject, www.es. emu.edu/~listen, www.soliloquylearning.com,** and **www.successforall.org/alphie's alley.**

Technology continues to play a larger and larger role in both instruction and assessment.

Some schools are experimenting with the use of individual hand-held devices that students use to answer multiple choice questions that instructors ask in class. The computer instantly tallies the responses, providing immediate feedback to the instructor about the students' understanding of the concepts just taught. These devices erase the need for a teacher to pick among a forest of waving hands and potentially overlook students with right answers—or students who are hopelessly lost. In addition to offering the ability for giving pop quizzes, these classroom response systems can also be used to take attendance, give more formal tests, and manage and run reports of students' assignments.

One important recent development is the use of technology to enhance the performance of teachers and tutors, not to replace them. This "lesson-**embedded technology**" has two forms.

- *Embedded multimedia* refers to video or DVD segments threaded into teachers' lessons, used to give students a clear mental image of the concepts being taught.
- *Computer-assisted tutoring* refers to computer software designed to help a human tutor work with struggling children, providing assessment, multimedia content, scaffolded practice activities, record keeping, lesson planning, and professional development.

A key attribute of lesson-embedded technology is the intention to help the teacher or tutor do a better job of teaching, rather than substituting for the human teacher. In fact, one explicit purpose of lesson-embedded technology is ongoing professional development for the teacher. The idea is that by showing *students* content and processes every day, *teachers* are also seeing them, and are receiving constant reinforcement of ideas they learned about in workshops. For example, in lessons involving cooperative learning, embedded multimedia can show cooperative groups working effectively on many objectives and in many contexts, clarifying for teachers as well as students exactly what students are expected to be doing in cooperative groups. The video can also model a playful but task-oriented affective tone within cooperative groups, and a focus on giving groupmates elaborated explanations rather than just answers (Webb & Palincsar, 1996).

embedded technology
Software and multimedia that is integrated into instruction in such a way that teachers or tutors can do a better job of teaching, because both they and their students receive reinforcement of content and concepts.

Similarly, embedded multimedia can show actors or puppets modeling use of metacognitive skills, talking through their thinking or problem-solving processes, or modeling creativity. Video threaded into daily lessons and tutoring sessions models the content in a compelling and pedagogically valid way, but more than this it gives both students and teachers daily visual models of how to effectively play their respective roles.

Lesson-embedded technology takes advantage of powerful cognitive effects of linked visual and auditory instruction. Mayer (2001) and his colleagues have demonstrated in dozens of experiments that combining visual content (still pictures or video) that reinforce text or auditory content greatly increases learning and retention. For example, research is increasingly finding that animations closely linked to text or auditory instruction greatly increase learning and retention (Hoeffler & Leutner, 2006).

Three year-long randomized experiments have evaluated outcomes of lesson-embedded technology in first grade reading. One (Chambers et al., 2006a) evaluated computer-assisted tutoring, one (Chambers et al., 2006b) embedded multimedia, and one a combination of the two (Chambers et al., in press). All three studies found that when well implemented, lesson-embedded multimedia significantly increased students' reading ability.

EMERGING RESEARCH IN NEUROSCIENCE

Over the past decade, significant new technologies such as magnetic resonance imaging have emerged that allow neuroscientists to look directly at brains in live, functioning individuals (Nicholson, 2006). In particular, functional MRIs, or fMRIs, allow us to look at changing pictures of the brain as individuals actually perform tasks, identifying which circuitry is "on line" during a particular activity (Wager, 2006). These methods have their limitations (Dumit, 2004; Uttal, 2001), but they provide a wonderful new tool for neuroscientists. Do they provide new perspectives for educators as well?

CONNECTIONS

See Ch. 6, pp. 177–179, for basic information on brain research, including fMRIs.

The answer is debatable. Willingham (2006) argues that, although neuroscience has been moving forward "in leaps and bounds," significant help for classroom teachers from these advances is still well in the future for most practical purposes. After all, he points out, while fMRI images might tell us which parts of a child's brain are active when she tries to read, that information doesn't really offer anything useful for that child's teacher. According to Willingham, "very exciting research is being conducted . . . Some of it is of interest to cognitive researchers trying to figure out how the brain works. And virtually all of it is far from being able to guide teachers."

Indeed, Willingham cautions against trying to apply emerging neuroscientific data directly to the classroom, rather than considering it as one piece of a very large cognitive puzzle. This caution is supported by the way in which such data has made its way into popular culture, and into the literature about teaching, over the past several decades. He points, for example, to research on left-brain vs. right-brain functions that is often used to support a variety of instructional strategies, although brain imaging data now confirms that both brain hemispheres participate in most cognitive tasks. He mentions as well the flurry of activity around providing stimulation for infants and young children, based on misinterpretation of data about stimulus-deprived subjects. Willingham does, however, see an immediate usefulness for neuroscientific findings in identifying children with learning disabilities, particularly dyslexia (see, for example, the work of Tallal and Gaab, 2006; Espy, Molfese, Molfese and Modglin, 2004; Lyytinen et al., 2005).

Despite any reservations about finding direct correlations between neuroscience and classroom teaching, we can nevertheless agree that psychological changes, behavioral changes, and changes in cognition as a consequence of learning, are all correlated with changes in the operation of the brain. We know something about *how* those changes occur, and we know something about *where* those changes occur. Neuroscience is on the cutting edge of behavioral science; it is supplying additional pieces of the cognitive puzzle all the time. As responsible educators, we should keep ourselves informed about this emerging data, and we should evaluate it thoughtfully and carefully for implications for teaching and learning. We might agree on three conclusions:

1. *Not all learning is equally likely.* Some things are easier to learn than other things. For instance, humans acquire language and are attuned to social stimuli. Some learning seems more *intuitive,* or easy: for humans, this kind of learning appears to include language (Pinker, 1994; 1997); understanding about objects and the behavior of objects in space (Rosser, 1994); the geometry of three-dimensional space and the natural number system (Gelman, 2006), and the distinction between living and non-living things (Inagaki & Hantano, 2006). Other learning can be *counterintuitive,* or hard to learn, and this appears to include mastering fractions, algebra, and Newtonian physics (Rosser, 2003), among other things.

This is not news, of course, to classroom teachers, who are probably very much aware that language and spatial relationships come more easily to young learners than advanced math concepts.

2. *Brain development constrains cognitive outcome.* One cannot alter a brain that is not yet ready for incoming experience to affect it. That is a point made years ago by Jean Piaget, who studied children's cognition, not their brains, and we now know that there is a correspondence between changes in the brain and cognitive development (Kuhn, 2006). While brain development takes place over a long time, *behavior change through learning cannot exceed the developmental status of the neural structure.*

Developmental research also suggests that cognitive accomplishment in children and adolescents is probably best conceptualized as *domain-specific.* Although the left and right hemispheres of the brain appear to participate together in most cognitive tasks, the brain is not entirely a *general problem solver* well adapted to all sorts of different challenges the person might encounter. It may be more accurate to envision the brain as a series of specialized problem solvers with specific regions or circuits well adapted to handling limited kinds of problems, such as way finding (a geometric problem solver), figuring out language (a linguistic problem solver), "reading" social information (a "people" problem solver).

As Willingham suggests, the classroom applicability of this is not yet clear, but future findings may uncover implications for teachers in stimulating particular domains to achieve particular goals.

3. *Some regions of the brain may be particularly important for cognitive outcomes, for supporting certain sorts of neural activities related to learning and cognition.* One region that has become a primary focus of much contemporary research is the prefrontal cortex. This region has been proposed as a mediator of behavioral planning and reasoning (Grafman, 1994), attentional processes (Foster, Eskes, & Stuss, 1994; Panskeep, 1998), the control of impulsivity (Murji & DeLuca, 1998; Rosser, Stevens, & Ruiz, 2006), and more recently, planning and executive cognitive functioning (Grafman, Spector, & Ratterman, 2005; Huey, Krueger, & Grafman, 2006), and even the ability to use rules when engaged in cognitive tasks (Bunge & Zelazo, 2006). In short, this appears to be the seat of what we think of as *deliberate cognitive activity,* what we try to encourage in the classroom.

Interestingly enough, this region is structurally immature even in adolescence. Gray matter in the frontal cortex peaks at about age 11 in females, at 12.1 years in males (Giedd, 2004; Giedd, Blumenthal, & Jeffries, 1999), while white matter volume in this region increases well into adulthood (Casey, Giedd, & Thomas, 2000). This is an area linked to the ability to inhibit impulses, to weigh consequences of decisions, to prioritize and strategize, in short, to act rationally. And it is still being remodeled well into early adulthood.

What does all this mean to the educator facing a classroom full of students? Given what we know about brain development and brain functioning, it means those recipients of instruction are *not* empty, unformed boxes waiting to be "filled up" with information, directions, and skills. It means they are not even finished boxes—that the receptacle itself is still changing and reforming. Learners are, in fact, neural works in progress, altering themselves with every new activity, every engagement, and every new skill acquired and fact learned. That remodeling is ongoing, protracted, and continuous. As neuroscience continues to provide a wealth of new data, and that data is woven together with the data provided by sociologists, behavioral scientists, psychologists, and educators, we may indeed find that brain research provides invaluable insights—and useful strategies—for us as educators.

Chapter Summary

What Has *No Child Left Behind* Accomplished?

After five years, the impact of *No Child Left Behind* federal legislation seems centered in three areas: curriculum emphasis; testing; and the roles played by federal, state, and local districts in the oversight of public education. More time is being spent in most schools on reading and math—the subjects most central to *NCLB*—and less on other subject areas. Students are taking more tests, and curricula are more aligned to standardized tests than in the past. Perhaps most significantly, the federal government has assumed a more primary role in public education than has been true in the past, and more responsibilities have devolved onto the states (although little funding has been made available for carrying out these responsibilities). Local school districts, traditionally the center of power in American education, have seen their control lessening. Finally, as a result of *NCLB,* more after-school and summer school programs are being offered for low-achieving students.

Accountability: The Pressure to Measure Progress

As educators at every level feel more and more pressured to demonstrate progress, some measures of progress appear to be open to potential contamination. Schools are instituting "teach to the test" curricula, for example, and students with disabilities are not always tested appropriately. Schools are implementing frequent benchmark assessments to insure that their students are prepared for standardized tests. Schools and districts are also looking more and more to testing data to make reforms to curriculum and instruction.

Why the Achievement Gap Isn't Closing, and How We Can Help

Despite the focus in *No Child Left Behind* on the progress of particular groups, the "achievement gap" between races, ethnic groups, and students at different socioeconomic levels shows no sign of closing. Some programs that have shown success in this area are instruction for English Language Learners (ELL), and non-school solutions—a focus, for example, on correcting vision and hearing problems—for disadvantaged children.

Emerging Applications of Technology

Technology continues to find new roles in the classroom. Among recent developments that show educational promise are simulations, hand-held technology and embedded multimedia. Hand-held devices allow students to answer questions simultaneously and for teachers to evaluate learning for all students, rather than relying on raised hands to identify students who understand and can respond. Embedded multimedia—video and DVD presentations threaded through content lessons—can provide visual stimuli for students in concept learning.

Emerging Research in Neuroscience

New tools like magnetic resonance imaging (MRI), and particularly functional MRI (fMRI), allow neuroscientists to see a brain at work—to identify what parts of the brain participate in particular tasks, including learning. The research emerging from the use of such tools is significant in moving us toward a more sophisticated understanding of the process of learning, but is not yet providing information of specific use to classroom teachers.

References

Adams, M. J. (2006). *Soliloquy Learning: Reading Assistant*. Retrieved October 20, 2006 from www.soliloquylearning.com.

August, D., & Shanahan, T. (Eds.) (2006a). *Developing literacy in second-language learners*. Mahwah, NJ: Erlbaum.

Amso, D. & Casey, B. J. (2006). Beyond what develops when: Neuroimaging may inform how cognition changes with development. *Current directions in psychological science*, Vol. 15, No. 1. February, 24–29.

August, D., & Shanahan, T. (2006b). Synthesis: Instruction and professional development. In D. August & T. Shanahan (Eds.), *Developing literacy in second-language learners* (pp. 351–364). Mahwah, NJ: Erlbaum.

Beck, J. E., & Mostow, J. (2005). *Mining data from randomized within-subject experiments in an automated reading tutor*. Paper presented at the annual meeting of the American Educational Research Association, Montreal, Canada.

Bernhardt, V. (2003). No schools left behind. *Educational Leadership, 60* (5), 26–30.

Bjorklund, D. F. & Pelligrini, A. D. (2001). *The origins of human nature: Evolutionary developmental psychology*. Washington, D.C.: American Psychological Association.

Bloom, B. S. (1976). *Human characteristics and school learning*. New York: McGraw-Hill.

Brooks-Gunn, J., & Duncan, G. J. (1997). The effects of poverty on children. *The Future of Children, 7* (2), 55–71.

Bunge, S. A., & Zelazo, P. D. (2006). A brain-based account of the development of rule use in childhood. *Current Directions in Psychological Science*. Vol. 15, No. 3, 118–121.

Carey, S. , & Gelman, R. (1991). *Epigenesis of mind: Essays on biology and cognition*. Hillsdale, NJ: Erlbaum.

Casey, B., Giedd, J. & Thomas, K. (2000). Structural and functional brain development and its relation to cognitive development. *Biological Psychology* 54, 241–257.

Chambers, B., Abrami, P. C., Tucker, B. J., Slavin, R. E., Madden, N. A., Cheung, A., & Gifford, R. (2006a). Computer-assisted tutoring in Success for All: Reading outcomes for first graders. Submitted for publication..

Chambers, B., Cheung, A., Gifford, R., Madden, N., & Slavin, R. E. (2006b). Achievement effects of embedded multimedia in a Success for All reading program. *Journal of Educational Psychology, 98*, 232–237.

Chambers, B., Slavin, R. E., Madden, N. A., Abrami, P. C., Tucker, B., J., Cheung, A., & Gifford, R. (in press). Technology infusion in Success for All: Reading outcomes for first graders. *Journal of Educational Psychology*.

Cheung, A., & Slavin, R. E. (2005). Effective reading programs for English language learners and other language minority students. *Bilingual Research Journal, 29* (2), 241–267.

Cooper, H., Charlton, K., Valentine, J. C., & Muhlenbruck, L. (2000). Making the most of summer school: A meta-analytic and narrative review. *Monographs of the Society for Research in Child Development* (Serial No. 260), 65 (1), 1–118.

Dede, C. (2006). *The River City project*. Retrieved October 20, 2006 from www.muve.gse.harvard.edu/rivercityproject.

Dumit, J. (2004). *Picturing personhood: Brain scans and biomedical identity*. Princeton, NJ: Princeton University Press.

Espy, K. A., Molfese, D. L., Molfese, V. J., and Modglin, A. (2004). Development of auditory event-related potentials in young children and relations to word-level reading abilities at age 8 years. *Annals of Dyslexia*, 54 (1), 9–38.

Fodor, J. A. (1983). *The modularity of mind*. Cambridge, MA: MIT Press.

Foster, J. K., Eskes, G. A., & Stuss, D. T. (1994). The cognitive neuropsychology of attention: A frontal lobe perspective. *Cognitive Neuropsychology,* 11, 133–147.

Francis, D., Lesaux, N., & August, D. (2006). Language of instruction. In D. August & T. Shanahan (Eds.), *Developing literacy in second-language learners* (pp. 365–414). Mahwah, NJ: Erlbaum.

GAO (1999). *Lead poisoning: Federal health care programs are not effectively reaching at-risk children. GAO/HEHS-99–18.* Washington, DC: Author.

Gelman, R. (2006). Young natural-number arithmeticians. *Current Directions in Psychological Science.* Vol. 15, No. 4, 193–197.

Giedd, J. N. (2004). Structural magnetic resonance imaging of the adolescent brain. In R. E. Dahl & L. P. Spear (Eds.) *Adolescent brain development. Vulnerabilities and opportunities.* Annals of the New York Academy of Sciences. Vol. 1021. New York: The New York Academy of Science.

Giedd, J. N., Blumenthal, J., & Jeffries, N. O. (1999). Cerebral cortical gray matter changes during childhood and adolescence: a longitudinal MRI study. *Nature Neuroscience,* 2, 861–863.

Gogtay, N., Giedd, J. N., Lusk, L., Hayashi, K. M., Greenstein, D., Vaituzis, A. S., Nugent, T. F., Herman, D. H., Clasen, L. S., Toga, A. W., Rapoport, J. L., & Thompson, P. M. (2004). Dynamic mapping of human cortical development during childhood through early adulthood. *Proceedings of the National Academy of Sciences, 101,* 8174–8179.

Gould, M., & Gould, H. (2003). A clear vision for equity and opportunity. *Phi Delta Kappan, 85* (4), 324–330.

Grafman, J. (1994). Alternative frameworks for the conceptualization of frontal lobe functions. In F. Boller & J. Grafman (Eds.), *Handbook of neuropsychology,* Vol. 9. San Diego: Elsevier.

Grafman, J., Spector, L., & Ratterman, M. (2005). Planning and the brain. In R. Morris & G. Ward (Eds.), *The cognitive psychology of planning.* Hove, England: Psychology Press, 181–198.

Harris, P. (2002). Learning-related visual problems in Baltimore City: A long-term program. *Journal of Optometric Vision Development, 33* (2), 75–115.

Heritage, M., & Chen, E. (2005). Why data skills matter in school improvement. Phi Delta Kappan, 86 (9), 707–710.

Hill, J. D., & Flynn, K. M. (2006). *Classroom instruction that works with English language learners.* Alexandria, VA: ASCD.

Hoeffler, T., & Leutner, D. (2006) Instructional animation versus static picture: A meta-analysis. Poster presented at the annual meeting of the *American Educational Research Association,* San Francisco, CA.

Huey, E. D., Krueger, F., & Grafman, J. (2006). Representations in the human prefrontal cortex. *Current Directions in Psychological Science.* Vol. 15, No. 4, 167–171.

Inagaki, K., & Hantano, G. (2006). Young children's conception of the biological world. *Current Directions in Psychological Science,* Vol. 15, No. 4, 177–181.

Jennings, J., & Rentner, D. S. (2006). Ten big effects of the No Child Left Behind Act on public schools. *Phi Delta Kappan, 88* (2), 110–113.

Kuhn, D. (2006). Do cognitive changes accompany developments in the adolescent brain? *Perspectives on Psychological Science.* Vol. 1, No. 1. 59–67.

Lauer, P. A., Akiba, M., Wilkerson, S., Apthorp, H., Snow, D., & Martin-Glenn, M. L. (2006). Out-of-school-time programs: A meta-analysis of effects for at-risk students. *Review of Educational Research, 76* (2), 275–313.

Lyytinen, H., Guttorm, T. K., Huttunen, T., Hämäläinen, J., Leppänen, P. H. T., and Vesterinen, M. (2005). Psychophysiology of developmental dyslexia: A review of findings including studies of children at risk for dyslexia. *Journal of Neurolinguistics,* 18, 167–195.

Mayer, R. E. (2001). *Multimedia learning.* New York: Cambridge University Press.

McComb, E. M., & Scott-Little, C. (2003). *After-school programs: Evaluations and outcomes.* Greensboro, NC: SERVE.

McGill-Franzen, A., & Allington, R. (2006). Contamination of current accountability systems. *Phi Delta Kappan, 87* (10), 762–766.

Mostow, J. (2006). *Project LISTEN.* Retrieved October 20, 2006, from www.cs.cmu.edu/~listen.

Murji, S., & DeLuca, J. W. (1998). Preliminary validity of the cognitive function checklist: Prediction of tower of London performance. *Clinical Neuropsychologist,* 12, 358–364.

National Institute of Child Health and Human Development. (2000). *Report of the National Reading Panel. Teaching children to read: an evidence-based assessment of the scientific research literature on reading and its implications for reading instruction: Reports of the subgroups* (NIH Publication No. 00–4754). Washington, DC: U.S. Government Printing Office.

Neisser, U., Boodoo, G., Bouchard, T, Boykin, W., Brody, N., Ceci, S., et al. (1996). Intelligence: Knowns and unknowns. *American Psychologist, 51,* 77–101.

Nicholson, C. (2006). Thinking it over: fMRI and psychological science. *Observer.* Vol. 19, No. 9, 20–25.

Northwest Evaluation Association. (2006, November). *Achievement gaps: An examination of differences in student achievement and growth.* Retrieved November 18, 2006, from http://www.nwea.org/assets/research/national/409_AchivGapStudyFinallowres_11106a.pdf

Panskeep, J. (1998). Attention deficit hyperactivity disorders, psychostimulants, and intolerance of childhood playfulness: A tragedy in the making? *Current Directions in Psychological Science.* Vol. 7, No. 3. 91–97.

Pinker, S. (1994). *The language instinct: How the mind creates language.* New York: Harper Collins.

Pinker, S. (1997). *How the mind works.* New York: Norton.

Popham, J. (2005). How to use PAP to make AYP under NCLB. *Phi Delta Kappan, 86* (10), 787–791.

Rosser, R. A. (1994). *Cognitive development: Psychological and biological perspectives.* Boston, MA: Allyn & Bacon.

Rosser, R. A. (2003). Scientific Reasoning. *Encyclopedia of Cognitive Science.* London: Nature Publishing Group.

Rosser, R. A. Stevens, S. & Ruiz, B. (2006). Cognitive markers of adolescent risk taking: A correlate of drug abuse in at-risk individuals. *The Prison Journal,* 85, 83–96.

Rothstein, R. (Ed.). 2004. *Class and schools: Using social, economic, and educational reform to close the black-white achievement gap.* Washington, DC: Economic Policy Institute.

Schmoker, M. (1999). *Results: The key to continuous school improvement.* Alexandria, VA: Association for Supervision and Curriculum Development.

Shanahan, T., & Beck, I. (2006). Effective literacy teaching for English language learners. In D. August & T. Shanahan (Eds.), *Developing literacy in second-language learners* (pp. 415–488). Mahwah, NJ: Erlbaum.

Shepard, L. A., & Smith, M. T. (Eds.) (1989). *Flunking grades: Research and policies on retention.* Philadelphia: Falmer.

Slavin, R. E., & Cheung, A. (2005). A synthesis of research on language of reading instruction. *Review of Educational Research, 75* (2), 247–284.

Slavin, R. E., & Madden, N. A. (Eds.) (2001). *One million children: Success for All.* Thousand Oaks, CA: Corwin.

Snow, C. (2006). Cross-cutting themes and future research directions. In D. August & T. Shanahan (Eds.), *Developing literacy in second-language learners* (pp. 631–632). Mahwah, NJ: Erlbaum.

Sousa, D. A. (2006). *How the brain learns.* 3rd ed. Thousand Oaks, CA: Corwin Press.

Starfield, B. (1997). A threat in the air. How stereotypes shape intellectual identity and performance. *American Psychologist, 52* (6), 613–629.

Tallal, P. and Gaab, N. (2006). Dynamic auditory processing, musical experience and language development. *Trends in Neurosciences,* 29, 382–390.

Uttal, W. (2001). *The new phrenology: The limits of localizing cognitive processes in the brain.* Cambridge, MA: MIT Press/Bradford Books.

Vaughn, R. D. (2003). Personal correspondence, April 22.

Wager, T. D. (2006). Do we need to study the brain to understand the mind? *Observer,* Vol. 19, No. 9, 24–27.

Webb, N. M., & Palincsar, A. S. (1996). Group processes in the classroom. N D.C. Berliner & R. C. Calfee (Eds.), *Handbook of Educational Psychology.* New York: Simon & Schuster Macmillan.

Whitman, S., Williams, C., & Shah, A. (2004). *Improving community health survey: Report 1.* Chicago, IL: Sinai Health System.

Willingham, D. T. (2006). Brain-based learning: More fiction than fact. *American Educator.* Fall 2006.

MyLabSchool Activities

CHAPTER 1: EDUCATIONAL PSYCHOLOGY: A FOUNDATION FOR TEACHING

Log onto Allyn & Bacon's MyLabSchool (www.mylabschool.com) and enter Assignment ID FDV1 into the Assignment Finder. Find and view the video *Becoming A Teacher*. In relation to what you've just seen in the video and what you've read in Chapter 1, answer the following questions.

1. The chapter notes that the best teachers are "intentional" teachers, critical thinkers who are constantly upgrading and examining their teaching practice. According to the chapter's descriptions and criteria, is Penny Brandenburg an "intentional" teacher?
2. What might Penny Brandenburg do to strengthen her teaching practices, according to the material in the chapter? What habits of mind, specific practices, and types of questions might Penny be asking herself?

CHAPTER 2: THEORIES OF DEVELOPMENT

Log onto Allyn & Bacon's MyLabSchool (www.mylabschool.com) and enter Assignment ID CMV4 in the Assignment Finder. Find and view the video called *Conflict Resolution*. In relation to what you've just seen in the video and what you've read in Chapter 2, answer the following questions.

1. According to research presented in this chapter, how people think about resolving problems is more important than the solutions they come up with. Based on Kohlberg's stages of moral reasoning described in the text, at what level of moral reasoning are the two children in this video who have the conflict?
2. To what stage is the peer mediator and the principal attempting to move the students? Why is this important, and potentially beneficial to them as students?

Now enter Assignment ID CS21 into the Assignment Finder. Scroll down to *A Look Inside: A Student Teacher's Dilemma*. Read the case and answer Question 1 raised at the end of it.

CHAPTER 3: DEVELOPMENT DURING CHILDHOOD AND ADOLESCENCE

Log onto Allyn & Bacon's MyLabSchool (www.mylabschool.com) and enter Assignment ID ECV1 in the Assignment Finder. Find and view the video called *Emotional Development in Toddlers*. In relation to what you've just seen in the video and what you've read in Chapter 3, answer the following questions.

1. The Slavin text says that a key goal of preschool, day care, and early intervention programs for toddlers is to help very young children develop a range of cognitive and emotional skills they will need to succeed in school. What are the central emotional skills being taught by teachers in this video clip?
2. How can parents and other caregivers help children develop the emotional skills necessary for school success?

Next enter Assignment ID EPRN in the Assignment Finder. Using Research Navigator, find Article 443331. How does the latest research on adolescent development challenge older theories of when adolescence begins and ends, as presented by Slavin?

CHAPTER 4: STUDENT DIVERSITY

Log onto Allyn & Bacon's MyLabSchool (www.mylabschool.com) and enter Assignment ID ELV2 in the Assignment Finder. Find and view the video titled *Involving Parents in the Educational Process*. In relation to what you've just seen in the video and what you've read in Chapter 4, answer the following questions.

1. What is happening at the O'Hearn School in Dorchester (outside of Boston) that the chapter says supports student success and engagement, especially among a diverse group of parents and learners?
2. What are the barriers to parental involvement that the O'Hearn School directly addresses? Specifically, how does the school invite parents to be involved in their children's educational experiences, and support parental inclusion?
3. Why does parental involvement matter, according to the research presented in this chapter?

CHAPTER 5: BEHAVIORAL THEORIES OF LEARNING

Log onto Allyn & Bacon's MyLabSchool (www.mylabschool.com) and enter Assignment ID SPV7 in the Assignment Finder. Find and view the video titled *ADHD*. In relation to what you've just seen in the video and what you've read in Chapter 5, answer the following questions.

1. What kinds of behavioral reinforcers are the teachers in Eric's program using to help Eric gain greater control of his behavior? As outlined by Slavin in this chapter, how are the concepts of behavioral shaping and extinction being used with this child with severe ADHD?
2. What are the limits of a behavioral approach to understanding the nature of Eric's difficulties? What does the evaluating psychologist say is bothering Eric, and how do the teachers use nonbehavioral theories and ideas to try to gain insight into his difficulties?

CHAPTER 6: INFORMATIONAL PROCESSING AND COGNITIVE THEORIES OF LEARNING

To explore the concepts in this chapter, you will watch two videos. Log onto Allyn & Bacon's MyLabSchool (www.mylabschool.com) and enter Assignment ID LAV4 in the Assignment Finder. Find and view the video titled *Mind Maps and Cooperative Learning*. In relation to what you've just seen in the video and what you've read in Chapter 6, answer the following questions.

1. How do the instructional strategies used by this teacher in this lesson support, or not support, Slavin's ideas about using metacognitive skills to help students learn?
2. Do you think students are effectively engaged by this exercise? Will they remember it, in your opinion?

Next, enter Assignment ID SSV2 in the Assignment Finder. Find and view the video titled *Teaching with Current Events*. In relation to this video and what you've read in Chapter 6, answer the following questions.

1. In terms of schema theory, how effectively is this teacher employing hierarchies of knowledge and students' background knowledge?
2. Do you think this is an effective discussion? Why or why not?

CHAPTER 7: THE EFFECTIVE LESSON

Log onto Allyn & Bacon's MyLabSchool (www.mylabschool.com) and enter Assignment ID GMV1 in the Assignment Finder. Find and view the video titled *Planning for Instruction*. In relation to what you've just seen in the video and what you've read in Chapter 7, answer the following questions.

1. Based on the principles outlined in this chapter, do the two teachers plan to use direct instruction in their presentation of the concept of AIDS? What evidence do you base your answer on?
2. Have the two teachers defined the learning objectives of this lesson? How will they check to see if students have learned what they've intended?
3. How are the two teachers planning for the transfer of learning of the concepts to students' real life?
4. Do you think the video demonstrates an example of effective lesson planning, based on the principles outlined by Slavin in this chapter? Why or why not?

CHAPTER 8: STUDENT-CENTERED AND CONSTRUCTIVIST APPROACHES TO INSTRUCTION

To explore the concepts in this chapter, log onto Allyn & Bacon's MyLabSchool (www.mylabschool.com) and enter Assignment ID SSV2 in the Assignment Finder. Find and view the video titled *Cooperative Learning*. In relation to what you've just seen in the video and what you've read in Chapter 8, answer the following questions.

1. Why are the teachers using small groups to explore the problems that beset the nation after the Civil War in this classroom? Is this a top-down processing instructional model, or a bottom-up one?
2. What are some examples in the video of the teachers scaffolding students' learning? Do you think the teachers are effective at shifting their level of intervention based on the student group's zone of proximal development?
3. Do you feel this is an effective cooperative learning exercise for teaching this content? Why or why not?

CHAPTER 9: ACCOMMODATING INSTRUCTION TO MEET INDIVIDUAL NEEDS

Log onto Allyn & Bacon's MyLabSchool (www.mylabschool.com) and enter Assignment ID CRV5 in the Assignment Finder. Find and view the video titled *Teaching Diverse Learners*. In relation to what you've just seen in the video and what you've read in Chapter 9, answer the following questions.

1. What strategies does the first teacher in this video say she uses to accommodate individual differences in achievement? What tools does she use to get to know students prior to planning instruction?
2. What does the second teacher say is a critical component of helping diverse learners, like English Language Learners, connect to reading and writing?
3. Based on the material in Slavin's chapter, what methods might the first teacher use to assist struggling learners in mastering material?

CHAPTER 10: MOTIVATING STUDENTS TO LEARN

To explore the concepts in this chapter, log onto Allyn & Bacon's MyLabSchool (www.mylabschool.com) and enter Assignment ID EPV6 in the Assignment Finder. Find and view the video titled *Motivating Through Problem Based Learning*. In relation to what you've just seen in the video and what you've read in Chapter 10, answer the following questions.

1. Compare the project-based learning exercises on the airport in the tape to Slavin's opening example in this chapter about a 10th grade history unit. Does Bill Meder's project in the videotape demonstrate the same motivational qualities that Cal Lewis's history unit does? Why or why not? Do the students in the tape seem intrinsically interested in the airport?
2. How might teacher Bill Meder, in the video tape, increase students' extrinsic motivation to work on the project about the airport? According to the principles in the chapter, would these intrinsic motivators be as effective as intrinsic ones?

CHAPTER 11: EFFECTIVE LEARNING ENVIRONMENTS

To explore the concepts in this chapter, you will watch two videos. Log onto Allyn & Bacon's MyLabSchool (www.mylabschool.com) and enter Assignment ID CMV3 in the Assignment Finder. Find and view the video titled *Defining Expectations*. In relation to what you've just seen in the video and what you've read in Chapter 11, answer the following questions.

1. Slavin emphasizes the importance of well-planned and engaging lessons as central to the prevention of misbehavior and the management of whole classroom behavior. Has the teacher in this clip planned the end of this lesson so that it is engaging to the class as a whole? Why or why not? Does the teacher experience any classroom management issues during the clip?

Now enter Assignment ID CMV2 in the Assignment Finder. Find and view the video titled *Field Trip*. Answer the following questions.

2. Does the teacher in this clip set class rules and expectations for the field trip effectively?
3. If you were a student in this class, would you be motivated to behave as she instructs? Why or why not?

CHAPTER 12: LEARNERS WITH EXCEPTIONALITIES

To explore the concepts in this chapter, log onto Allyn & Bacon's MyLabSchool (www.mylabschool.com) and enter Assignment ID SPV2 in the Assignment Finder. Find and view the video titled *The Inclusive Classroom*. In relation to what you've just seen in the video and what you've read in Chapter 12, answer the following questions.

1. Slavin explains how a classic experiment on inclusion demonstrates that students with learning differences tend to do better in regular education environments. When you watch this tape, are you aware of the students with special needs? Do you think they are being well supported in this instructional environment? Why or why not?
2. The two teachers in this room are working cooperatively to meet the needs of the students. Does this help to create a powerful instructional environment for all learners? Why or why not? What is your evidence?

CHAPTER 13: EFFECTIVE LEARNING ENVIRONMENTS

To explore the concepts in this chapter, you will watch two videos. Log onto Allyn & Bacon's MyLabSchool (www.mylabschool.com) and enter Assignment ID EPV8 in the Assignment Finder. Find and view the video titled *Criteria for Evaluation*. In relation to what you've just seen in the video and what you've read in Chapter 13, answer the following questions.

1. In the video, why does James Popham say it is important for children to develop their own internal evaluative criteria?
2. Does Slavin emphasize the same principles?

Next, enter Assignment ID GMV6 in the Assignment Finder. Find and view the video *Portfolios*. Answer the following questions.

3. How is the portfolio assessment in this clip different from standardized testing? Why might this be considered more "authentic" evaluation than other kinds of tests?
4. In your opinion, is portfolio assessment best used for formative or summative evaluation? Why?

CHAPTER 14: STANDARDIZED TESTS

To explore the concepts in this chapter, log onto Allyn & Bacon's MyLabSchool (www.mylabschool.com) and enter Assignment ID EPV8 in the Assignment Finder. Find and view the video titled *Standardized Tests*. In relation to what you've just seen in the video and what you've read in Chapter 14, answer the following questions.

1. What are the problems with using standardized tests to assess learning and achievement that Gerald Bracey outlines? Why does he say that ice skating is an easier activity to judge and score than mathematics, for instance?
2. What are some of the test taking skills demonstrated by the teachers in the videos? Why is it important in the current climate to develop "test wise" kids?
3. What are some of the problems that Slavin, and the video, identify with using standardized tests to assess the overall educational quality of a school?

CHAPTER 15: CURRENT ISSUES AND EMERGING TRENDS

To explore the concepts in this chapter, log onto Allyn & Bacon's MyLabSchool (www.mylabschool.com) and enter Assignment ID ETV in the Assignment Finder. Find and view the video called *Drill and Practice*. In relation to what you've just seen in the video and what you've read in Chapter 15, answer the following questions.

1. Slavin describes the kinds of changes schools are making to instruction and in classroom preparation for tests, due to new forms of accountability and scrutiny of numerical data on student performance under NCLB. Do you think the ways in which the teacher is using the multiplication website in the first part of this video is instructionally useful and appropriate? Why or why not? Will the kinds of practice students get with multiplication tables be useful in raising performance on state-mandated tests?

2. In the second portion of the video, when the teacher is using a website to help students review state capitals, are the guidelines for powerful "lesson-embedded technology" being followed, as outlined by Slavin in this chapter? Why or why not? How instructionally valuable do you think the use of technology is for the children in this class? Explain your answer.

Notes

Notes

Notes

Notes

Notes

Notes

Notes

Notes

Notes

Notes

Notes

Notes